CLOCK IN THE JUNGLE

Written by
KETKI PANDIT

Illustrated by
SNEHA UPLEKAR

talking CUB
An Imprint of Speaking Tiger Books

TALKING CUB
Published by Speaking Tiger Books LLP
4381/4, Ansari Road, Daryaganj
New Delhi 110002

First published in paperback in Talking Cub by Speaking Tiger Books in 2021
Text copyright © Ketki Pandit 2021
Illustrations copyright © Sneha Uplekar 2021

ISBN: 978-93-90477-01-2
eISBN: 978-93-90477-97-5

10 9 8 7 6 5 4 3 2 1

For Abiir, Ayra, Viha, Yashodhan and all the
future custodians of our beautiful planet.

We thank Saili Palande Datar for sharing
her love and knowledge of the Western Ghats.

Who sets an alarm
early morning for the birds?
Maybe there's a clock
hiding deep in the jungle?

At seven-thirty a.m.
does it tick in the meadows
as sundews swallow bugs
and ants march in crooked rows?

Or perhaps it hangs
by a green vine snake
basking in the gentle sun
of 9 a.m.

Wonder if the giant squirrel
knows it's ten past ten.
Does she keep a time-keeper
in her leafy den?

In the gleaming sun
a purple frog checks
his reflection,

schools of fish go wading by
at half-past eleven.

Can you tell the time
on the clock by this ant hill?

Is it time for lunch yet
for mum and dad hornbill?

A lazy lull falls on the jungle,
the clock strikes two-thirty.
Who is that keeping a watch
perched high on a tree?

Cutting through the stillness,
'ROAR!' comes a mighty cry.
Monkeys jump and deer run
and birds begin to fly!

The queen of the jungle cools off.
No creature ventures close.

Cautious, from a distance,
they watch her as she goes.

At twilight shadows lengthen,
evening is on its way.
Can you tell what time
river otters come to play?

Sun sets and darkness falls,
a tinge of orange lingers.
Creatures of the night
get ready for adventures.

12
11
10
9
8
7
6
5
4
3
2
1

Sky aglow with countless stars,
fireflies in trees.
What's the time when slow lorises
snooze in the gentle breeze?

It's long past your bedtime,
wild boars are on the prowl—
digging for some juicy worms,
can you hear them growl?

28

they roll up into scaly balls
so they don't get caught.

Viper snake takes a stance,
his scary fangs unfold...
In a matter of seconds
the mouse is in his hold.

12
1
2
3
4
5
6
7
8
9
10
11

At 3 a.m. the jungle
echoes with barks and howls:
chirping crickets, hissing snakes,
and of course, hooting owls!

12
11
10
9
8
7
6
5
4
3
2

Frogs as large as your palm
and small as a fingernail
flying off tree branches,
hopping on leafy trails.

Stirring in their dew-drenched nests,
birds chirrup at dawn.
Soon the sun will rise again
and jungle-life goes on.

Chasing time in cycles
the clock keeps ticking away...
it looks a lot like yesterday
but today's a brand new day!

Wondering where the plants and animals
in this book come from? They are all natives
of Western Ghats in India, ancient mountains
that are older than the Himalayas!

These mountains are covered by thick forests
that are home to a wide variety of plants, birds,
animals and insects; many of which are not
found anywhere else in the world! That's why the
Western Ghats are a global biodiversity hotspot
and also a UNESCO World Heritage Site.

Let's find these creatures in the book!

1. A sundew plant eating bees

2. A weaver bird weaving its nest

3. A giant squirrel feasting on a mango

4. A hornbill feeding his mate

5. A monkey dozing off on a tree

6. A deer sharpening its horns on a tree trunk

7. A bison watching otters play in the river

8. A colourful snail resting on a tree bark at night

9. Pangolins eating ants with their long, sticky tongues

10. A tiger resting by a pond

Answer Key: Page Numbers
(1) 7 (2) 14 (3) 9 (4) 13 (5) 15 (6) 23 (7) 21 (8) 35 (9) 28 (10) 18

Ketki is a restless animal in the concrete jungle of Mumbai, India—always planning her next escape into the wilderness. She is a graduate of Film and TV Institute of India and New York University. She spends her time reading, writing, making films, teaching screenwriting and fussing over her potted plants.

Sneha writes, draws and makes films, and is a graduate of the National Institute of Design, India. When she is not tinkering with words and pictures, she is fangirling over turtles (the best animals to exist!). Sneha lives in Bristol, UK, with her partner and a (almost) pet fox. But really, she lives in the forest inside her head.